My Bars

Cover Photography by Michael Thaxton Photography
Facebook.com/michaelthaxtonphotos
Instagram.com/mthaxton83

©2019
Vivid Dreams Publishing
Virginia Beach, VA
Rochester, NY
Facebook.com/vividdreamspublishing
ISBN: 9781674433332

www.ingramcontent.com/pod-product-compliance
Lightning Source LLC
Chambersburg PA
CBHW070630220526
45466CB00001B/137